Leonardo da Vinci

and the RENAISSANCE

D0870204

CONTENTS

ANDREW LANGLEY

What's in your Treasure Chest?

Your treasure chest is packed full of exciting activities! There is a replica of Leonardo's flying machine to construct; a slide-pull version of The Last Supper, *both before and after restoration; Brunelleschi's Cathedral Dome to assemble; a Renaissance timeline, and a facsimile of Leonardo's notebook sketches.*

Construct a fully-operational model of Leonardo's flying machine, nicknamed "The Great Bird."

Leonardo's Flying Machine Model

In the tray are the pieces to make up a model of Leonardo's amazing flying machine. Fit the pieces together following the diagrams and written instructions, and your pilot will be in place, ready to operate the wings of the flying machine. Move the pilot's arms and legs to raise and lower the wings, which are attached to the wooden handles the pilot holds. Leonardo based his designs on detailed studies of the flight of birds—although it is believed that his model never actually flew because the materials he specified were too heavy!

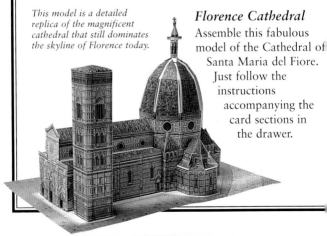

This model is a detailed replica of the magnificent cathedral that still dominates the skyline of Florence today.

Florence Cathedral

Assemble this fabulous model of the Cathedral of Santa Maria del Fiore. Just follow the instructions accompanying the card sections in the drawer.

A timeline poster featuring people, places, and events during Leonardo's life.

Timeline

Open the drawer to find a wall poster that chronicles Leonardo's life. Historical dates are also listed so you can see how world events unfolded during the Renaissance.

Facsimile Sketchbook

Look at these images from Leonardo's notebooks, and you'll see that he was an engineer, scientist, architect, and anatomist, as well as being a superb artist.

An introduction to the many 'faces' of the great Master.

Punched Cartoon Sketch

In your drawer you'll find a punched cartoon. Dust powdered charcoal through the holes onto the surface below, and you are left with a transferred outline of the image from which to paint your picture.

A punched cartoon, like the one that Leonardo could have used in preparation for his fresco The Last Supper.

Last Supper Slider

Pull the tab to see Leonardo's masterpiece before and after restoration.

Marvel at the difference careful restoration can make to a painting with this pull-tab version of The Last Supper.

The Last Supper By Leonardo Da Vinci 1498

The Alberti Grid

Grids like this were used by Leonardo and his contemporaries to ensure that their paintings were in perspective.

Use the plastic grid attached to the lid of your pack to help make your drawings accurate.

Who was Leonardo da Vinci?

Leonardo was born near the Italian village of Vinci, not far from Florence. He is always known by the name of his birthplace—Leonardo da (of) Vinci. His father, Piero, was a local official and his mother, Caterina, was probably a servant in his father's household. Piero and Caterina never married each other, and from the age of five, young Leonardo lived with his father.

How medieval artists saw Christ: a mosaic in Monreale Cathedral, Sicily.

In 1452, the year in which Leonardo was born, everyday life in Europe had scarcely altered in 500 years. The vast majority of people still worked on the land, and there were very few large towns. The hugely powerful Catholic Church still took 10% (a tithe) of what everybody earned.

Despite this, important changes were taking place in the world: guns and explosives were taking over from medieval castles and knights in armor, the ancient Christian city of Constantinople in the East was about to fall to the armies of Islam, and a golden age for the arts was beginning—a period we call the Renaissance (meaning "re-birth.")

The unchanging landscape of the Tuscan countryside, with peasants at work harvesting grapes for winemaking.

The young Leonardo was very handsome and graceful. He was probably the model for Verrocchio's statue of David.

Country Boy

Young Leonardo would have known little about these great events. He grew up in the Tuscan countryside, surrounded by vineyards, olive groves, flowers, and animals. The boy later wrote that his earliest memory was of lying in his cradle when a huge black hawk swooped down, touching his mouth with its tail. Like the village peasants, he later saw this as an omen that he was meant for greatness.

Dragon Painter

It was soon clear that Leonardo had amazing artistic talent. One day his father asked him to paint a picture on a wooden shield, as a gift for a peasant. He was expecting something simple, but the boy had other ideas. Using lizards, insects, and bats as his models, he painted a terrifying dragon with gaping jaws.

When Piero saw the finished picture, he realized that it was something special. He bought the peasant a cheap, ready-painted shield, then secretly sold Leonardo's work to a merchant in Florence for 100 ducats—a huge sum. The merchant sold it later on for 300 ducats.

The Move to Florence

A view over the city of Florence today, showing clearly the round dome of the Cathedral and, next to it, the tall thin bell tower, or campanile. In the foreground is the Arno river.

"He was always setting himself to learn many things, only to abandon them almost immediately." This is how Vasari, a Renaissance writer, described Leonardo's early schooling. Drawing, arithmetic, singing, carving—he tried them all, only to discover that he soon knew more than his tutors.

In about 1466, the family moved to Florence, and Piero looked around for the very best art teacher for his son. He arranged that Leonardo should enter the workshop of Andrea del Verrocchio, one of the most famous artists of the day. Here he would learn the basic skills of painting and sculpture, and other fine arts such as goldsmithing and drawing.

Florence and the Medici

At this time, Florence was growing rich and powerful, thanks to the profits made by its bankers and craftsmen. The city was actually a tiny self-governing state. Its citizens (tradesmen who belonged to one of the 21 "guilds" or societies) elected their own leaders and councils, which in turn made most of the laws.

Leonardo in his master's workshop. Artists and decorators had plenty of work in Florence's booming economy

Lorenzo de' Medici, nicknamed "the Magnificent," whose family dominated Florence.

Under the control of the Medici family, Florence had become a center not only for money and trade, but also for Italy's greatest artists and designers. The Medici and other wealthy families paid vast sums of money for new buildings, paintings, and sculptures to make their city

more beautiful. There were more than 200 workshops devoted to painting, goldsmithing, and carving. Leonardo himself tried his hand at town planning, illustrating his ideas for an "ideal city" set out in checkerboard fashion, criss-crossed by canals and elevated walkways, with plenty of parks and squares, and an underground sewage system.

The emblem of the Medici family

City-States

Fifteenth-century Italy did not have one overall ruler. Most of the poorer, southern part was governed from Naples, while the pope controlled the central area around Rome. The north of Italy was the richest region, with fertile farmland and easy access to other European countries. Like Florence, the north was split up into several city-states, each with its own ruler. Milan was famous for armor and metalwork, Urbino for pottery, and Venice for glassware. There was often great competition between these cities, and the strongest (such as Milan) sent armies of mercenary soldiers to attack their rivals.

The Italian city-states were famous for producing valuable, ornate glassware and tableware.

Back to the Past

The Arch of Titus in Rome. Ancient Roman civilization had a great influence on Renaissance learning.

"Verrocchio was amazed to see what extraordinary beginnings Leonardo had made," wrote Florentine art historian, Vasari. The young artist was already about 16 years old when he started his training in the workshop. But he had probably spent little time at any school, preferring to roam the countryside and listen to the peasants' stories.

Few children went to school in those days, because their families needed their help with the crops and animals in the fields. Boys who were going to be priests were sent to classes in monasteries or cathedrals, where they were taught to read and write. They also learned many prayers and Bible passages by heart.

Renaissance Learning

Leonardo was living in exciting times because ideas about art, education, and government were changing fast. Scholars were rediscovering the ancient civilizations of Greece and Rome, with their great buildings, sculptures, and poetry, as well as writings on law and politics. By studying these ancient ideals, thinkers found a fresh way of looking at the world. Historians later named this change a "renaissance," or "re-birth" of learning.

The Annunciation *by early Renaissance artist, Fra Angelico. Notice how the decorated columns resemble ancient Roman architecture.*

The huge vault of the Pantheon in Rome, built about 125A.D.

The Great Dome

These new ideas also inspired artists and architects. They studied the sculptures and buildings created by the ancient Romans and decided to imitate them.

When architect Filippo Brunelleschi visited Rome, he was fascinated by the Pantheon, a vast, circular temple built in about 125A.D. It had a dome on top which spanned a gap of more than 43 yards without any internal supports. Nothing as daring as this had been constructed before.

Brunelleschi measured the Pantheon carefully, and returned home to Florence. He was determined to design a similar dome, which would be added as the finishing touch to the city's new cathedral. Many people believed that this was impossible. Without a supporting framework, they said, the dome would simply collapse. But Brunelleschi proved them wrong: he designed a dome to crown the Cathedral of Santa Maria del Fiore, and in 1436 his great new building towered over the city.

The dome of Florence Cathedral, designed by Brunelleschi and inspired by the Pantheon. The copper globe on top was cast in Verrocchio's workshop.

At Home

Leonardo was entered as an independent master in the register of the Guild of St. Luke when he finished his apprenticeship in 1472. He was 20 years old.

We do not know where Leonardo lived when he was a young apprentice in Florence. He probably stayed at home with his father, or joined Verrocchio's household. At this time, craftsmen usually used their homes as workplaces, or workshops, and anyone who worked for them lived as part of the family.

For most people, except for the very poor, houses were much more comfortable than they had been in the Middle Ages. Glazed windows kept out the drafts, and fireplaces with chimneys replaced the smoking hearth in the middle of the room. Lamps gave better light, mirrors gave clearer reflections, and clocks kept time more accurately.

Food and Drink

The choice of food in the late fifteenth century was much more limited than it is today. No European had yet traveled to the American continent, and so Leonardo would never have tasted foods such as potatoes, tomatoes, coffee, or chillies. He would have eaten mostly fresh fruits and vegetables, as well as meat, rice, and pasta.

To preserve meat and fish for the winter, people dried it in the sun or pickled it in salt. Water was too unclean to drink on its own. Most people mixed wine with the water to kill the germs—or simply drank wine on its own. Nearly every Italian peasant, or householder, had enough garden space to grow their own grapes for wine-making every fall.

The Borgias were one of the wealthiest families in Italy. This painting, by a Victorian artist, shows what luxurious clothes they could buy.

Dressing Up

Leonardo was fond of fine clothes, and cut a dashing figure as he strode about Florence with his rose-colored tunic, flowing cloak, and long blonde hair. Indeed, rich people of the time loved to show off in costumes made of the most expensive materials—silk robes, fur collars, and velvet gowns. Women used different kinds of cosmetics to whiten their teeth, or redden their cheeks. They shaved or plucked their eyebrows, and took immense care in arranging their hair, bleaching it in the sun, and glueing curls to their foreheads.

Kitchen staff bustle to prepare food for their master's dinner.

Trade and Wealth

A Florentine cloth merchant shows off his wares—including silks and satins.

"Often when he was walking past the places where birds were sold he would pay the price asked, take them from their cages, and let them fly off into the air, giving them back their lost freedom." Vasari's touching description of Leonardo shows that he was a familiar sight at the market stalls of Florence.

L eonardo would have seen a huge variety of goods for sale. Besides the local fruits, vegetables, meats, and cheeses, the stores would have displayed silk and satin cloth, and gold and silver ornaments made by the city's smiths. There would have been beautiful leatherwork from Spain, and iron and tin goods from Britain, as well as the famous woolen cloth woven in Florence itself.

As sailors pushed into unexplored regions, map-makers were able to produce more detailed maps of the world.

Merchant Adventurers

During the fifteenth century, European sailors traveled further and further from home. Most of them were merchants, eager to open up new trade routes, and expand their markets overseas. They aimed to reach the most exotic and profitable market of all—the lands of China, Japan, and Ceylon (Sri Lanka) in the Far East, where they could buy precious cargos, such as silks and spices.

Portuguese explorers edged along the west coast of Africa until they rounded the southern tip (the Cape of Good Hope). From here, Vasco da Gama sailed east to India in 1498. Meanwhile, the Spanish had been exploring westward. In 1492, Christopher Columbus had crossed the Atlantic to reach islands off the coast of America—the "New World."

Christopher Columbus, the Genoese explorer whose voyage across the Atlantic was backed by the Spanish king and queen.

Money Lenders

The richest of all the city's traders were the bankers. Families such as the Medici had made their fortunes by lending sums of money which were repaid to them with interest. They lent money to merchants to buy foreign goods or build workshops, and to kings and nobles who wanted to hire soldiers to fight their wars. Some bankers also worked for the pope. They collected his tithes (taxes) from Catholic churches all over Europe. The tithes came in every shape and kind—furs, crops, wool, even whalebone from Iceland. The bankers sold these goods (at a profit, of course) then paid the proceeds to the pope.

Spices such as cinnamon, nutmeg, cloves, and mace, brought from faraway countries, were worth their weight in gold.

The New Painting

"Submit yourself to the direction of a master for instruction as early as you can; and do not leave the master until you have to." These are the words of Cennino Cennini, an artist in Florence who wrote a guide for apprentice painters in about 1400.

Hand-made brushes and pigments, such as ultramarine and orange, were the materials of Renaissance artists.

A Renaissance artist had to learn his craft the hard way. Leonardo's first jobs in his master Verrocchio's workshop would have been to sweep up, to fetch and carry, and to grind rocks and other materials to make pigments (colorings) for paint. Then he would be instructed in drawing and painting, as well as in making brushes, preparing paints, and using gold leaf.

Pioneer Painters

In the Middle Ages, artists had painted religious subjects. Their works had a Christian message and they were not concerned with making their pictures lifelike. But from the early fourteenth century, painters in Florence began to depict people and objects more naturally. The earliest of these painters was Giotto, whose graceful frescos (paintings on damp plaster) showed realistic figures displaying real emotions. Later artists such as Masaccio, went even further and painted massive, realistic people in natural settings. Leonardo must have seen Masaccio's powerful, expressive pictures in the nearby Brancacci Chapel.

A detail from The Betrayal of Christ *by Giotto (1267–1337), a pioneer of Renaissance painting.*

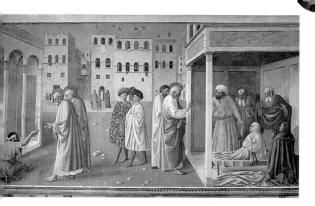

Part of Masaccio's great series of wall paintings in the Brancacci Chapel in Florence.

Light and Perspective

It soon became clear that Leonardo had an exceptional talent. By 1480, he was a master painter working for himself alone, and producing religious works such as the *Annunciation*, and his first portrait (of Florentine beauty Ginevra de' Benci). These paintings show his amazing skill in painting the effects of light and shade.

Leonardo was also fascinated by perspective—a mathematical way of showing a three-dimensional object on a flat surface. His studies, based on geometry, helped to prove that parallel lines meeting at a "vanishing point" at eye-level create the illusion of space to the viewer. He even designed a "perspectograph" to help him trace the outlines of an image on glass.

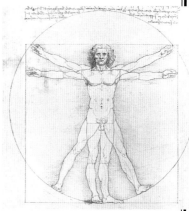

Leonardo's skill in geometry is shown in this drawing of the proportions of the human body.

Powerful Patrons

Leonardo's fame spread quickly, and he knew how to make the most of it. In 1482 he sent a letter to the wealthy ruler of Milan, Ludovico Sforza, offering his services as painter, architect, sculptor, and builder of bridges and weapons.

A design for a domed church drawn by Leonardo in about 1488.

S oon afterward, he was invited to the Milanese court. According to Vasari, Leonardo "took with him a lyre (a stringed instrument) that he had made himself, mostly of silver, in the shape of a horse's head." Ludovico was impressed, not just by the music, but also by his visitor's outstanding talent. For the next 17 years, he paid Leonardo to take on a huge number of projects.

Leonardo dreamed up this early idea for an armored vehicle, which could carry eight men.

Marvels in Milan

Working for a rich and powerful patron was very pleasant. Leonardo was free to wander the grounds of Milan castle as well as the palace itself, which employed more than 200 servants. In return, he designed buildings, cloth-weaving looms, metal-rolling mills, cannons, and dozens of other machines. He also drew up plans for a new city complete with roads and drains. To celebrate Ludovico's son's wedding, Leonardo invented an amazing series of devices, including a

The tower and inner courtyard of Sforza Castle in Milan, where Leonardo lived in the 1490s.

giant egg which opened to reveal models of the planets, and the signs of the Zodiac!

Unfinished Masterpiece

By the mid-1480s, inventions seemed to interest Leonardo more than art. Yet he still found time to set up his own artist's workshop in Milan and to take on pupils. He also painted several of his greatest works. Among these are the portrait of a Milanese beauty, *Lady With an Ermine*, and *The Virgin of the Rocks*.

The Virgin of the Rocks.

Leonardo's grandest idea was for a gigantic statue of Ludovico's father astride a horse. This would be cast in bronze, and stand nearly 26 feet high. It would have been, said a friend, "the most stupendous and glorious work ever made." He produced many drawings, ordered 7 tons of bronze, and even fashioned a clay model, but the statue itself was never completed.

This ambitious design for a giant horse and rider posed many problems for Leonardo, and he never made the finished statue.

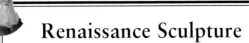

Renaissance Sculpture

"Sculpture is a simpler form of statement than painting, and needs less mental effort" wrote Leonardo. He made fun of the sweaty sculptor, whose *"face is covered with paste and all powdered with marble dust, so that he looks like a baker. His house is dirty and filled with chips and stone dust."*

W e know very little about Leonardo's work in sculpture. He clearly thought it was a lower kind of art than painting, and none of his sculpted works have survived. Yet around him sculptors were producing some of the finest works of the Renaissance.

Michelangelo Buonarroti (1475–1564), one of the greatest geniuses of Renaissance Italy, was not just a sculptor but also a painter, an architect, and a poet.

Mighty Michelangelo

The first great Italian sculptor was Donatello, who used the inspiration of Greek and Roman sculpture to show the grace and beauty of the human body. Verrocchio himself was famous for his bronze castings, and produced the thrilling statue of the mercenary soldier, Colleoni, on horseback. But the greatest of them all was Michelangelo Buonarroti. His massive nude statue of David (completed in 1504) is the best-known piece of

Michelangelo's famous statue of David.

sculpture in the world, full of grandeur, strength, and energy.

Like Leonardo, Michelangelo had a huge range of other talents in painting, architecture, engineering, and poetry. The two great artists were hired to paint battle scenes for the city hall in Florence, but the works were never finished.

St. Peter's Church in the Vatican City, Rome, was originally planned in the form of a Greek Cross, with four arms of equal length around a central dome.

Balance and Harmony

The rediscovery of the ideas of the ancient Greeks and Romans had a huge influence on Renaissance artists. For a start, they learned that beauty and harmony could be created by studying mathematics. They shaped their

statues according to geometric rules, and the natural proportions of the human body, which they saw as a reflection of God's perfect universe.

Artists also became fascinated with the myths of the classical world. They began to depict gods, goddesses, heroes, nymphs, and other legendary creatures, as well as strictly Christian subjects.

The massive figure of Moses, carved by Michelangelo for the tomb of Pope Julius II.

Working for the Church

In 1494, Leonardo was hired to paint a mural (a wall picture) for a convent in Milan. The subject was the Last Supper taken by Jesus and his followers. Although the work began well, after many months it was still not finished.

Leonardo painted his Last Supper high on a wall in the dining area. His use of perspective made it look like another room.

The prioress of the convent was impatient at the delay, and complained to Ludovico Sforza. When Ludovico asked Leonardo why he was so slow, he protested that it was because he spent hours every day in the city's slums—at work on the mural. The Duke was puzzled, but Leonardo explained that he went there to look at people's faces. He was searching for one that was villainous enough to use as a model for the face of the traitor, Judas.

Grand church decorations from the High Renaissance— carved pulpit, stained glass window, and sculpted figures.

Papal Patrons

The Catholic Church paid artists to produce thousands of religious works of art during the Renaissance. These ranged from stained-glass windows and carved pulpits, to paintings for altars and sculpted figures. The subjects were saints, martyrs, the Virgin Mary and, of course, Christ Himself. In an age when few people could read, churches played the part of picture books and art galleries. Although the subjects rarely changed, the vision

Leonard's study of the head of the disciple Judas, made for the Last Supper.

of the artists grew bolder and less traditional. They showed warm and believable figures instead of the remote, idealized forms of the Middle Ages. The people in their paintings showed normal human emotions, and were seen smiling, laughing, frowning, or crying.

The Sistine Chapel

The two most astonishing religious works of the period were by Leonardo and his archrival, Michelangelo. Leonardo's *Last Supper* was completed at last in about 1498, and was immediately hailed as a masterpiece. His stunning use of perspective draws the viewer's eye into the picture, even though it is well above eye level.

Michelangelo took on an even more gigantic task— to paint the ceiling of the Sistine Chapel in Rome. Starting in 1508, he spent more than four years creating frescos which showed The Creation and Noah's Flood. He had to work lying on his back for much of the time, yet produced images of haunting beauty and power. Michelangelo later added pictures of The Last Judgement on the altar wall of the chapel.

The amazing sweep of Michelangelo's frescos on the Sistine Chapel ceiling.

The Written and Printed Word

An illuminated 12th century Bible. Before the invention of the printing press, Bibles were rare, and were found only in monasteries or in the houses of the rich.

The greatest invention of the Renaissance was the printing press. The Chinese had devised a form of printing four centuries before Leonardo's birth, but the idea had never reached the West. All through the Middle Ages, monks or professional scribes had copied out books by hand. This system was very slow and it could take a whole year to produce a single copy of a long book. So books were scarce and very valuable. It was no wonder that very few people could read.

In about 1450, a German craftsman built the first European printing press. His name was Johannes Gutenberg, and he based his machine on the grape-crushers (presses) used to make wine. He used movable pieces of type (one for each letter) made of cast metal.

A printed book and the press which printed the pages. The screw on the press was turned to squeeze the inked type onto the paper.

Reading for All

The new printing process was much quicker and cheaper than hand-copying and for the first time in history, books could be produced in large numbers. Gutenberg's first complete, printed book was an edition of the Bible, which he published in 1455.

Soon hundreds of print shops sprang up throughout Europe. They produced everything from religious and classical works to poetry, pamphlets, and popular stories. Suddenly, books were easily available for everyone, and many more people learned to read. Pictures could be printed, too, so that an artist's work could be seen all over Europe.

A page from the Bible printed by Johannes Gutenberg.

Leonardo's Notebooks

Leonardo had a very unusual handwriting style. From his childhood, he wrote with his left hand and started his lines on the right-hand side of the page. The result was a "mirror" of ordinary script. For letters and official notes, he had to write in the normal way, but he found this difficult.

Leonardo filled thousands of pages of notebooks with his peculiar writing. These notebooks are crammed full with his ideas and inventions, as well as drawings and designs. He covered an astounding range of topics, including art, science, the planets, the human body, warfare, and natural history.

Leonardo's unusual handwriting style can be clearly seen in this page from his notebooks.

The Human Body

In the 1480s, Leonardo began yet another major project. He decided he would study and illustrate how the different systems of the human body worked, from blood circulation and breathing, to digestion and the muscles. There was only one way to do this—to cut up dead bodies.

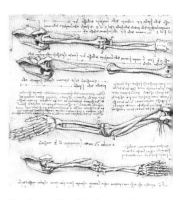

Detailed studies of the bones and joints of the human arm and hand—part of Leonardo's painstaking project.

It was an unpleasant job. Hot weather made the corpses rot quickly, so Leonardo had to work at night in a dank cellar lit by candles. With a cloth covering his mouth and nose to keep out the smell, he dissected about 30 bodies. He wrote later of his "fear of living through the night hours in the company of these corpses, quartered and flayed and horrible to behold."

Unsophisticated early medicine: a doctor scorches or "cauterizes" the wounds of a plague victim with a red hot iron.

The New Anatomy

Very few people had ever dared to dissect corpses before. The leaders of the Catholic Church disapproved of the activity, because they thought it mocked God's creation. All through the Middle Ages, doctors had learned their craft from books. They knew very little about how the human body really worked.

Artists such as Leonardo and Michelangelo, who wanted to be able to depict muscles and bones accurately, pioneered this work. They were followed by doctors who studied human organs and body systems. This new knowledge helped them to treat wounds and diseases more effectively.

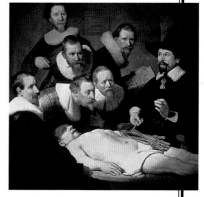

The Anatomy Lesson by Dutch artist, Rembrandt. Until the late 16th century, the Church discouraged the dissection of corpses.

A Dangerous Age

For many people living in 1500, death was never far away. Throughout Europe, half of all babies died before they were a year old, and the average life-span was little more than 30 years. Many deadly diseases raged across Europe, the worst being the plague which had killed millions since it first appeared in 1348. The threat of warfare, violence, and starvation was also ever present. Although most big cities had hospitals, often paid for by rich merchants or by the Church, they could do little.

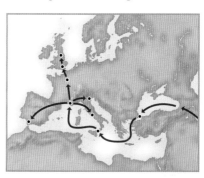

Map showing the spread of the plague, or "Black Death," from the East.

Renaissance Warfare

Armored horsemen ride into battle in 16th century Italy.

"I have bombardment devices which hurl rocks as thickly as hailstones, creating great terror in the enemy with their smoke." These were some of the weapons promised by Leonardo in his letter to Ludovico Sforza in 1482. He also boasted of schemes for attacking fortified walls, digging tunnels, and draining castle moats.

It may seem strange that a trained artist should spend his time dreaming up such things, but warfare was a central part of life in the unstable world of Renaissance Italy. There were many wars between cities and states, as well as the threat of invasion from outside.

Weapons Galore

The art of war was taken very seriously. Artists were also fine craftsmen, and their talents and knowledge were useful to military leaders. Giotto, and later Michelangelo, were employed to design strong walls and forts to defend the city of Florence against attack. Sculptors were hired to cast cannons because of their skill with metals.

A panoramic painting of the city of Siena, showing the walls fortified against attack.

Military machines: Leonardo's gruesome design for two chariots with scythes on the wheels. The blades could be lifted to avoid cutting one's own troops.

But no one had such amazing ideas as Leonardo. He drew plans for new types of cannons—including one which sprayed iron bolts over a wide area, and another with three rows of barrels which were fired one after another. He designed lightweight bridges and ladders for troops to cross rivers, or climb castle walls. He even depicted an armored vehicle—400 years before the first battle tanks.

Invaders from the North

In 1494, the king of France marched into northern Italy. His aim was to conquer Naples in the south, but on the way he attacked Florence and Rome. In Milan, Ludovico Sforza helped to form an alliance against the invaders, but he was soon defeated and his city was seized by the French. Leonardo now had no patron and was forced to flee. After short stays in Mantua and Venice, he returned to Florence in 1500.

Portrait of Francis I, King of France, who invaded northern Italy in 1494.

New Horizons

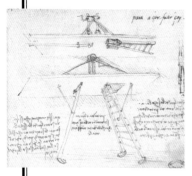

One of several flying machines designed by Leonardo, which had four wings and used foot power.

The Renaissance was an age of discovery. Artists were discovering new ways of expressing their ideas, and scientists were discovering more about earth sciences and how the human body worked. Travelers were discovering parts of the Earth where no European had ever been before.

By 1513, Portuguese sailors had not only rounded Africa's southern cape, but also explored the Congo river. Others had set up trading posts in the South China sea. Sebastian Cabot had reached Hudson Bay in North America, while the Spaniard Vasco Balboa was the first European to catch sight of the Pacific Ocean when he climbed a tree in Panama to see the lay of the land.

Up in the Air

Leonardo was an artist who was also a scientist, and he was determined to push back the barriers of what people could do. It might have seemed impossible that humans could fly, but that did not stop him dreaming and planning. By carefully studying the flight of birds, he was able to design a pair of wings, made of cloth, wood, and leather. We shall never know whether he ever tried out his ideas.

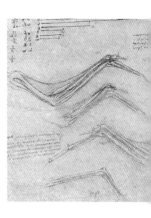

Leonardo made many studies of the wings and flight muscles of birds.

We cannot be sure that Leonardo ever actually constructed his flying model, but inside your pack you will find the pieces to make up a fabulous working model, based on Leonardo's own designs.

Was Leonardo also an explorer? During the 1480s he wrote an account of a journey to the East "somewhere in Asia." He describes the terrible sea voyage to get there, the vast mountains and forests, and the mysterious cities. There is nothing to prove that he actually made this trip—the story could have come from his restless imagination.

Out of this World

Leonardo also studied the heavens. He tried to work out how far away the Sun was from Earth, and realized that the Moon's light was really reflected from the Sun. But he still accepted the ancient view that the Earth was at the center of the universe.

Meanwhile, in Poland, another scientist was setting out to change this belief. Nicolaus Copernicus was beginning a 30-year project which would inspire a new and shocking theory—that the Sun was at the center of the solar system, and that the Earth and the other planets moved around it. This discovery changed the whole course of astronomy.

The layout of the universe, as imagined by Copernicus, with the Sun at the center.

Renaissance Man

*After leaving Milan, Leonardo wandered from city to city. He worked in Florence again where he completed two of his greatest paintings—*The Virgin and Saint Anne *and* The Mona Lisa. *Leonardo returned to Milan in 1507, then moved to Rome in 1513. In Rome he was employed by a member of the powerful Medici family.*

With her mysterious smile and beautiful features, The Mona Lisa is one of the best-known portraits ever painted. Nobody knows who the lady really was.

L eonardo's final move was to France. In 1516, King Francis I invited him to live near the court at Amboise. The artist was now partially paralyzed, but he could still draw and helped to plan grand celebrations at the palace. He died in France on May 2, 1519, and was buried at Amboise. "When I thought I was learning to live," he once wrote, "I was learning to die."

Universal Men

Leonardo also believed that "a painter is not admirable unless he is universal"—he must try to consider everything. Certainly there was no Renaissance figure more nearly universal than Leonardo himself. His interests covered an incredible range and included painting, architecture, botany, astronomy, mathematics, flight, fables, music, and constructing everything from canals and gardens to cranes and giant catapults.

Leonardo was a fine player of the lira da braccia, above, as well as a skilled singer.

Queen Elizabeth I of England, the greatest monarch of the age.

But he was not the only "Renaissance Man." There was also his rival, Michelangelo, King Francis I of France, a skilled soldier and a lover of the arts, and England's King Henry VIII, a fine swordsman, singer, and astronomer. There were Renaissance Women too, notably Queen Elizabeth I of England, who could speak several languages, ride all day, and dance better than her courtiers.

Dürer's portrait of himself, completed in 1498.

The Spread of the Renaissance

The Italian Renaissance also inspired many artists and scholars in the northern part of Europe. Many, such as the painters Hans Holbein, Pieter Brueghel, and Albrecht Dürer, traveled to Italy to study the new ideas and techniques. When they returned home, they carried the influence with them. As a result, northern cities, such as Paris, Nuremberg, and London, became thriving centers of trade and culture during the sixteenth century.

A map of Paris in 1572: it became one of the great cities of the age as the Italian Renaissance spread north.

Leonardo's Legacy

"Marvelously endowed by heaven with beauty, grace and talent in such abundance that he leaves other men far behind"—that was how Vasari judged Leonardo. Leonardo's drawings and paintings astonished people during his lifetime. Onlookers crowded to see his sketches, and even marveled at his unfinished pictures.

Even the simplest of Leonardo's drawings are revered as stunning works of art. Many were lost, and some, such as this, remained unfinished.

The admiration for Leonardo's works of art has continued ever since. In the 1800s, Napoleon wanted to remove the *Last Supper* from its wall in Milan, fix it to a frame, and take it to France. Today, *The Mona Lisa* (in the Louvre Museum, Paris, France) is the most visited painting in the world—so famous that it has to be protected by a bulletproof window.

It took longer for Leonardo's other works to be as admired. Most of his notebooks lay neglected for nearly 200 years, and did not reach a wide audience until about 1900. Then they showed the world that, not only was Leonardo a supreme master of Renaissance art, but a pioneer of science and engineering, whose ideas were far ahead of their time.

The Louvre in Paris, France, the modern home of Leonardo's greatest painting.

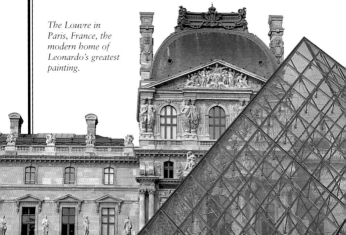